CHILDREN'S MINISTRY CLIP ART BOOK

COMPILED BY LINDA MATTIA

Featuring the art of:
Rick Bundschuh, Curt Dawson, Tom Finley, Dennis Jones, Catherine Leary, Jim Padgett,
Bron Smith, Joyce Thimsen, Chris Wilson and Chizuko Yasuda.

Gospel Light

HOW TO MAKE CLEAN COPIES
FROM THIS BOOK

You may make copies of portions of this book with a clean conscience if:

- you (or someone in your organization) are the original purchaser;
- you are using the copies you make for a noncommercial purpose (such as teaching or promoting your ministry) within your church or organization;

- you follow the instructions provided in this book.

However, it is ILLEGAL for you to make copies if:

- you are using the material to promote, advertise or sell a product or service other than for ministry fund-raising;
- you are using the material in or on a product for sale;
- you or your organization are **not** the original purchaser of this book.

By following these guidelines you help us keep our products affordable.

Thank you,
Gospel Light

CONTENTS

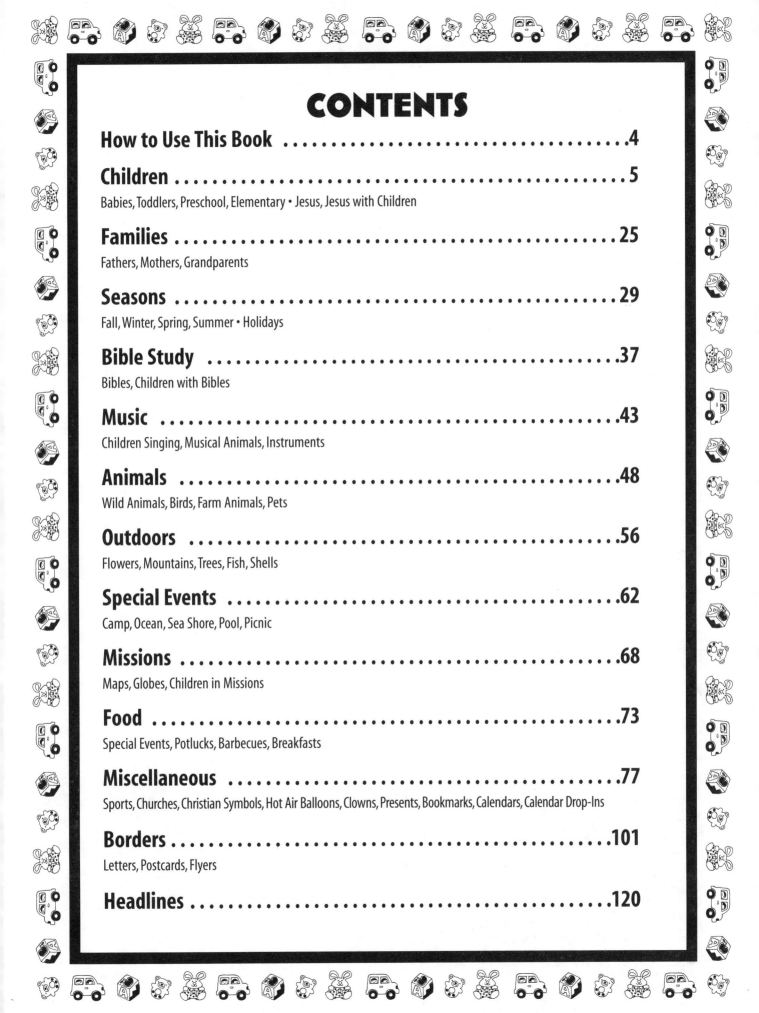

HOW TO USE THIS BOOK

Collect These Tools and Supplies:

✓ Photocopy machine and paper
✓ Transparent tape, rubber cement or glue stick
✓ Scissors

OPTIONAL:
✓ Typewriter and paper

Follow These Easy Steps:

1. Cut out the artwork and copy. You may want to enlarge or reduce artwork and/or copy if you have access to a photocopier with that capability. Optional: Type additional copy on a piece of white paper.

2. Decide where to position the art and your copy. Either make a few pencil sketches on scratch paper or decide in your mind the basic arrangement you will use. Plan to leave a one-half inch (or more) margin on your paper.

3. Tape, glue or use rubber cement to attach the artwork and all copy to a sheet of white paper. (Lines may be caused by the edges of paper you've glued to your final copy. Prevent lines by taping all edges.)

4. Make as many copies as you need.

CHILDREN

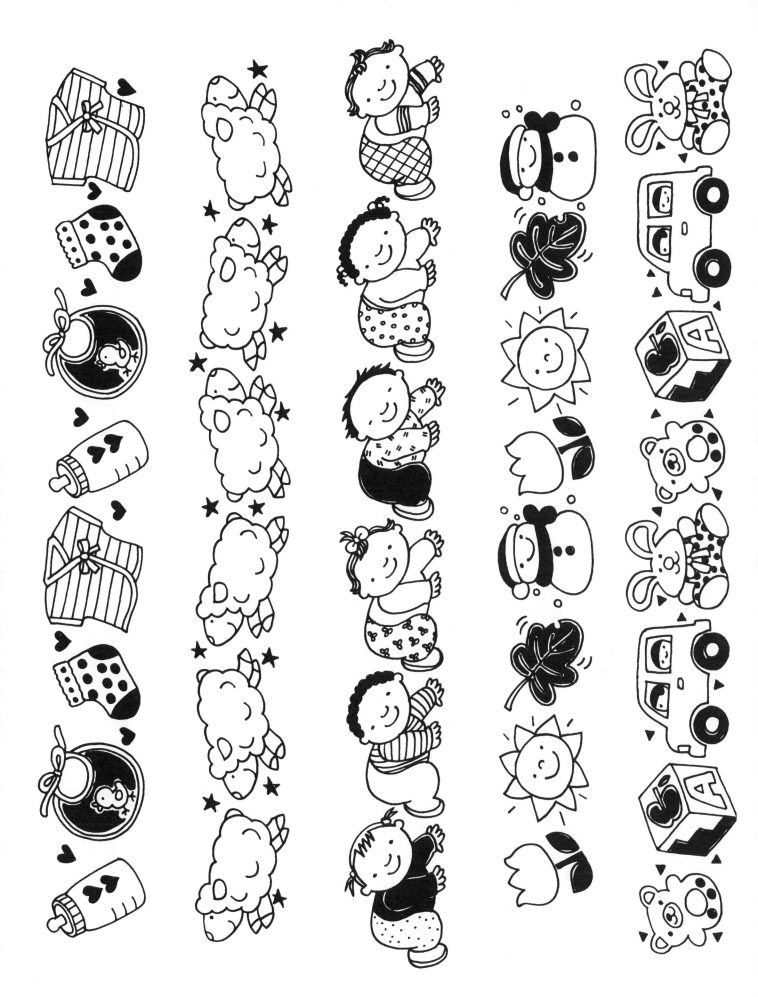

FAMILIES

SEASONS

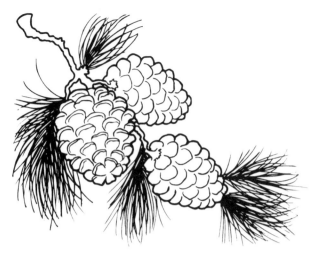

BIBLE STUDY

MUSIC

ANIMALS

OUTDOORS

8 × 5 =
2 × 6 =

SPECIAL EVENTS

MISSIONS

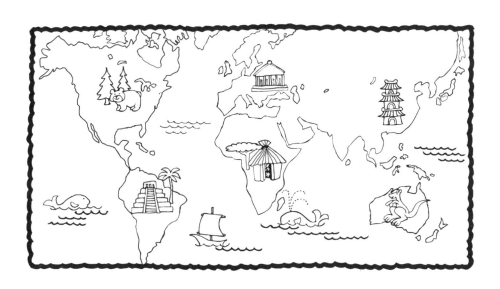

FOOD

MISCELLANEOUS

Up and Away

God, We give you thanks.
1 Chronicles 29:13

Be kind and compassionate to one another.
Ephesians 4:32

GOD IS MY HELPER!

God made the world
See Acts 17:24

God is with you wherever you go.

See Joshua 1:9

Every-thing God Made Is Good

see Genesis 1:31

GOD, WE GIVE YOU THANKS.

1 CHRONICLES 29:13

Sing praises to the Lord.

Psalm 9:11

Monday	Tuesday	Wednesday	Thursday
Friday	Saturday	Sunday	

JANUARY	January
FEBRUARY	February
MARCH	March
APRIL	April
MAY	May
JUNE	June
JULY	July
AUGUST	August
SEPTEMBER	September
OCTOBER	October
NOVEMBER	November
DECEMBER	December

New Year's Day	New Year's Day
Martin Luther King's Birthday	Martin Luther King's Birthday
Lincoln's Birthday	Lincoln's Birthday
Ash Wednesday	Ash Wednesday
Valentine's Day	Valentine's Day
Presidents' Day	Presidents' Day
Washington's Birthday	Washington's Birthday
St. Patrick's Day	St. Patrick's Day
Palm Sunday	Palm Sunday
Good Friday	Good Friday
Easter	Easter
Daylight Saving Time Begins	Daylight Saving Time Begins
Passover	Passover
National Day of Prayer	National Day of Prayer
Mother's Day	Mother's Day
Memorial Day	Memorial Day
Flag Day	Flag Day
Father's Day	Father's Day
Independence Day	Independence Day
Labor Day	Labor Day
Columbus Day	Columbus Day
Daylight Saving Time Ends	Daylight Saving Time Ends
Halloween	Halloween
Election Day	Election Day
Veterans Day	Veterans Day
Thanksgiving Day	Thanksgiving Day
Hanukkah	Hanukkah
Christmas Day	Christmas Day

1 2 3 4 5 6 7 8 9 10 11 12 13 14 15 16 17 18 19 20 21 22 23 24 25 26 27 28 29 30 31

1 2 3 4 5 6 7 8 9 10 11 12 13 14 15 16 17 18 19 20 21 22 23 24 25 26 27 28 29 30 31

1 2 3 4 5 6 7 8 9 10 11 12 13 14 15 16 17 18 19 20 21 22 23 24 25 26 27 28 29 30 31

1 2 3 4 5 6 7 8 9 10 11 12 13 14 15 16 17 18 19 20 21 22 23 24 25 26 27 28 29 30 31

1 2 3 4 5 6 7 8 9 10 11 12 13 14 15 16 17 18 19 20 21 22 23 24 25 26 27 28 29 30 31

1 2 3 4 5 6 7 8 9 10 11 12 13 14 15 16 17 18 19 20 21 22 23 24 25 26 27 28 29 30 31

1 2 3 4 5 6 7 8 9 10 11 12 13 14 15 16 17 18 19 20 21 22 23 24 25 26 27 28 29 30 31

1 2 3 4 5 6 7 8 9 10 11 12 13 14 15 16 17 18 19 20 21 22 23 24 25 26 27 28 29 30 31

	SUNDAY	MONDAY	TUESDAY	WEDNESDAY	THURSDAY	FRIDAY	SATURDAY

JULY

AUGUST

SEPTEMBER

OCTOBER

NOVEMBER

DECEMBER

FALL

Winter

Christmas

VALENTINE'S DAY

E·A·S·T·E·R

SUNRISE SERVICE

Groundhog Day

THANKSGIVING

4th of July

Spring!

Camp Out

PICNIC

POOL PARTY

FATHER'S DAY

BEACH PARTY

SUMMER!

Pizza Party

FUN NIGHT

MOVIE NIGHT · Action!

MISSIONS

GROUP MEETING

Hooked on the Bible · HOLY BIBLE

TRIP

Join Together

Don't Miss It!

JESUS

LEADERSHIP MEETING

Children's Musical

WORK DAY

HEY LOOK!

 Get Together!

 PARTY

 Happy Birthday

 MOTHER'S DAY

 BIBLE

 Bring Your Friends!

 Two BY Two!

 Drama

 PRAYER MEETING

 Sunday School

 MEETING

 Awards Night

 HIKE!

 TEACHER'S MEETING

 Bible Study

 Graduation

 HELPING HANDS

 RING! Don't Forget!

 Car Wash

 Junk Sale

 PotLuck

BORDERS

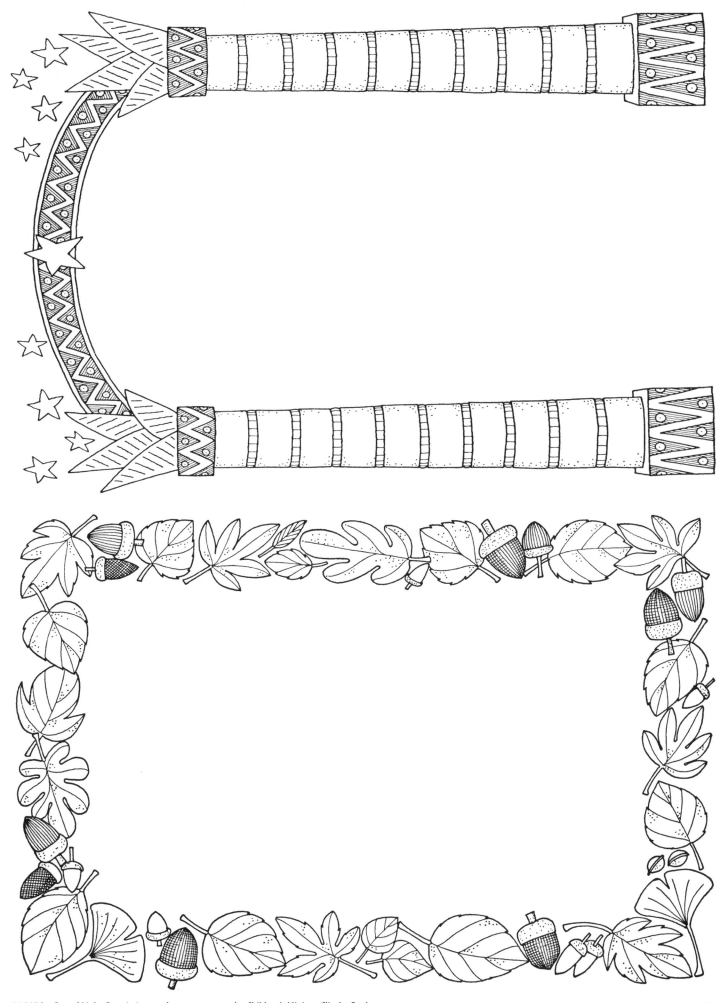

Hey, Kids!

HEADLINES

Look What's New!

Smart Sunday School Helps
from Gospel Light

Grow Your Own Sunday School.

A ton of reproducible resources to help you recruit and motivate leaders and teachers, promote support within the congregation and increase attendance at Sunday School.

Sunday School Promo Pages
By Wes and Sheryl Haystead
Manual • ISBN 08307.15894

Hundreds of Bright Ideas for Children's Workers.

Advice, answers and articles on every aspect of teaching children. Reproducible so that you can give training to all of your teachers, volunteers and parents.

Sunday School Smart Pages
Edited by Wes and Sheryl Haystead
Manual • ISBN 08307.15215

Bible Skits for All Occasions.

52 lively reproducible Bible-theme skits in each book. Each skit includes director's tips, Bible background information and group discussion questions. Less than 33¢ per skit!

Big Book Bible Skits
Manual • ISBN 08307.19164

Here's a Colorful Way to Bring the Bible to Life!

Here's a great way to introduce Bible learning while the kids are busy with their crayons includes 116 verses in both NIV and KJV translations. These reproducible pages can be used again and again.

Bible Verse Coloring Pages
Coloring Book • SPCN 25116.06720

Hundreds of Smart Ideas for 5th and 6th Grade Sunday School.

Here's a life-saving resource that puts the most current articles, tips, and quick solutions for teaching 5th and 6th graders. Use these reproducible pages for training or teacher refreshment. The perfect companion for any brand of curriculum.

5th & 6th Grade Smart Pages
Manual • ISBN 08307.18052

Holiday Programming Just Got Easier!

Take the anxiety out of planning, staging and presenting programs for Advent, Christmas, Easter, Thanksgiving, Mother's Day and more. Includes 23 wide variety skits for all ages. Reproducible.

Holiday Skits
Manual • ISBN 08307.17781

Fun Games that Teach Kids About the Bible.

200 reproducible Bible learning games. Fun, active games for 1st through 6th graders to help review Bible stories, reinforce Bible memory verses and apply them to a child's life.

Big Book of Bible Games
Manual • ISBN 08307.18214

Give Your Kids the Best Parties!

This easy-to-use resource provides decorating ideas, clip art, fun snack recipes, great games and activities and much more! Great for all children's programs, including special events, day camps, Sunday School, VBS, Christian schools and home birthday parties.

The Big Book of Theme Parties, Snacks and Games
Manual • ISBN 08307.18206

Bible Memory Music Kids from Six to Sixty Will Love.

Every word of these upbeat songs is straight from the Bible. It's the ultra-cool way to memorize the scriptures being studied in Gospel Light's 5th and 6th grade Sunday School curriculum, Planet 56! And it's reproducible–so you can make copies for all your kids.

The Bible in Your Brain Scripture Memory Music Vol. 2
Reproducible Cassette • SPCN 25116.09584
Reproducible CD • SPCN 25116.10264

Instant Art for Your Church.

These popular books include Bible verses, borders and hundreds of reproducible illustrations to help you create professional bulletins, flyers, posters and more. Complete with simple instructions.

Big Picture Bible Time Line
ISBN 08307.14723

Complete Bible Story Clip Art Book
ISBN 08307.13859 OOS

Sunday School Clip Art Book
ISBN 08307.11147

Make Any Bible Lesson Come to Life!

Hand puppets grab your kids attention and help them remember your lesson. Use them at home, in Sunday School, VBS and anytime you want a child's full attention. Includes reproducible patterns and guidelines to make your job easier.

Lofty the Bird Puppet
Hand Puppet • UPC 607135.001522

Paka the Lion Puppet
Hand Puppet • SPCN 25116.09029

Easy-to-Make Puppets and How to Use Them
Manual • ISBN 08307.16793

Craft Ideas for Creative Lessons.

Crafts make ideal teaching activities. Each of these crafts include step-by-step instructions, illustrations and patterns using economical and easy-to-find materials.

High Adventure Crafts for Kids
ISBN 08307.18516

Celebrating Our Families–Crafts for Kids
ISBN 08307.16750

Safari Crafts for Kids
ISBN 08307.17684

Bible Times Crafts for Kids
ISBN 08307.15967

Mountain Crafts for Kids
ISBN 08307.14766

Pioneer Crafts for Kids
ISBN 08307.14235

Country Crafts for Kids
ISBN 08307.16106

Handcraft Encyclopedia
ISBN 08307.14901 OOS

202 Things to Do
ISBN 08307.00269 OOS

Best-selling Clip Art You Can Use on Your Computer.

Bible Story Clip Art on disk
Windows • SPCN 25116.08952
Macintosh • SPCN 25116.08944

Kid's Worker's Clip Art on disk
607135.001546 CD ROM

Sunday School Clip Art on disk
607135.002598 CD ROM
Macintosh • SPCN 25116.08960

Summer Ministries Clip Art on disk
Windows • SPCN 25116.10248
Macintosh • SPCN 25116.10221

Church Bulletin Clip Art on disk
607135.001560

Keep Track of Kids with Attendance Resources.

These resources make record keeping simple and efficient. Each large, colorful Attendance Chart lets you keep track of your students for over two months. Give kids Peel 'n Press stickers so they can measure their weekly attendance!

Hot-Air Balloon Theme Attendance Chart
SPCN 25116.09916

Farm Theme Attendance Chart
SPCN 25116.05279

Island Theme Attendance Chart
SPCN 25116.04868

Pioneer Theme Attendance Chart
SPCN 25116.04876

Attendance Cards
SPCN 25116.02806 (Pack of 100)

Class Record Book
SPCN 25116.01656

Class Report Envelope
SPCN 25116.02822 (Pack of 10)

Offering Envelopes
SPCN 25116.02156 (Pack of 50)

Teacher Certificate
SPCN 25116.02180 (Pack of 10)

VBS Registration/Attendance Cards
SPCN 25116.02199

Visitor's Registration Slip
SPCN 25116.02849

STICKERS

Bible Characters Stickers
UPC 607135.000839

Alpine Wildlife Stickers
SPCN 25116.01664

Frontier Life Stickers
SPCN 25116.04760

High Country Plants & Flowers Stickers
SPCN 25116.01672

Pioneer Trappin's Stickers
SPCN 25116.04744

Prairie Animals Stickers
SPCN 25116.04752

Christian Symbols Stickers
SPCN 25116.04779

Beach Toys Stickers
SPCN 25116.05767

Cars and Trucks Stickers
SPCN 25116.07328

City Animals Stickers
SPCN 25116.07344

Friendly Neighbors Stickers
SPCN 25116.07336